Reasons To Be A Yankees Fan

An Intelligent Guide

Max Hater

The most thoroughly researched and coherently argued fan guide to date, "Reasons To Be A Yankees Fan: An Intelligent Guide" is a fan dissertation sure to provide vital data to help you make an educated fan decision . Lawmakers require that we state the book is mostly blank and contains precisely 1600 words. In other 'words', it's a gag gift, but also a must-have addition to any fan or hater's coffee table.

"Juuuuuust a bit outside!"

-Bob Uecker

www.MaxHater.com

ISBN-13: 978-1544864259
ISBN-10: 1544864256

DEDICATION

This guide is dedicated to all the true fans and haters out there.
Without you, this book wouldn't be possible!

TABLE OF CONTENTS

1 TEAM HISTORY

Our analysis has found no reasons to be a fan, based on their team history!

Our analysis has found no reasons to be a fan, based on their team history!

Our analysis has found no reasons to be a fan, based on their team history!

Our analysis has found no reasons to be a fan, based on their team history!

Our analysis has found no reasons to be a fan, based on their team history!

Our analysis has found no reasons to be a fan, based on their team history!

Our analysis has found no reasons to be a fan, based on their team history!

Our analysis has found no reasons to be a fan, based on their team history!

Our analysis has found no reasons to be a fan, based on their team history!

Our analysis has found no reasons to be a fan, based on their team history!

Our analysis has found no reasons to be a fan, based on their team history!

2 FRONT OFFICE

Our analysis has found no reasons to be a fan, based on their front office!

Our analysis has found no reasons to be a fan, based on their front office!

Our analysis has found no reasons to be a fan, based on their front office!

Our analysis has found no reasons to be a fan, based on their front office!

Our analysis has found no reasons to be a fan, based on their front office!

Our analysis has found no reasons to be a fan, based on their front office!

Our analysis has found no reasons to be a fan, based on their front office!

Our analysis has found no reasons to be a fan, based on their front office!

Our analysis has found no reasons to be a fan, based on their front office!

Our analysis has found no reasons to be a fan, based on their front office!

Our analysis has found no reasons to be a fan, based on their front office!

3 COACHES

Our analysis has found no reasons to be a fan, based on their coaches!

Our analysis has found no reasons to be a fan, based on their coaches!

Our analysis has found no reasons to be a fan, based on their coaches!

Our analysis has found no reasons to be a fan, based on their coaches!

Our analysis has found no reasons to be a fan, based on their coaches!

Our analysis has found no reasons to be a fan, based on their coaches!

Our analysis has found no reasons to be a fan, based on their coaches!

Our analysis has found no reasons to be a fan, based on their coaches!

Our analysis has found no reasons to be a fan, based on their coaches!

Our analysis has found no reasons to be a fan, based on their coaches!

Our analysis has found no reasons to be a fan, based on their coaches!

4 PLAYERS

Our analysis has found no reasons to be a fan, based on their players!

Our analysis has found no reasons to be a fan, based on their players!

Our analysis has found no reasons to be a fan, based on their players!

Our analysis has found no reasons to be a fan, based on their players!

Our analysis has found no reasons to be a fan, based on their players!

Our analysis has found no reasons to be a fan, based on their players!

Our analysis has found no reasons to be a fan, based on their players!

Our analysis has found no reasons to be a fan, based on their players!

Our analysis has found no reasons to be a fan, based on their players!

Our analysis has found no reasons to be a fan, based on their players!

Our analysis has found no reasons to be a fan, based on their players!

5 PERSONNEL

Our analysis has found no reasons to be a fan, based on their personnel!

Our analysis has found no reasons to be a fan, based on their personnel!

Our analysis has found no reasons to be a fan, based on their personnel!

Our analysis has found no reasons to be a fan, based on their personnel!

Our analysis has found no reasons to be a fan, based on their personnel!

Our analysis has found no reasons to be a fan, based on their personnel!

Our analysis has found no reasons to be a fan, based on their personnel!

Our analysis has found no reasons to be a fan, based on their personnel!

Our analysis has found no reasons to be a fan, based on their personnel!

Our analysis has found no reasons to be a fan, based on their personnel!

6 STADIUM

Our analysis has found no reasons to be a fan, based on their stadium!

Our analysis has found no reasons to be a fan, based on their stadium!

Our analysis has found no reasons to be a fan, based on their stadium!

Our analysis has found no reasons to be a fan, based on their stadium!

Our analysis has found no reasons to be a fan, based on their stadium!

Our analysis has found no reasons to be a fan, based on their stadium!

Our analysis has found no reasons to be a fan, based on their stadium!

Our analysis has found no reasons to be a fan, based on their stadium!

.

Our analysis has found no reasons to be a fan, based on their stadium!

7 FANS

Our analysis has found no reasons to be a fan, based on their fans!

Our analysis has found no reasons to be a fan, based on their fans!

Our analysis has found no reasons to be a fan, based on their fans!

Our analysis has found no reasons to be a fan, based on their fans!

Our analysis has found no reasons to be a fan, based on their fans!

Our analysis has found no reasons to be a fan, based on their fans!

Our analysis has found no reasons to be a fan, based on their fans!

Our analysis has found no reasons to be a fan, based on their fans!

Our analysis has found no reasons to be a fan, based on their fans!

Our analysis has found no reasons to be a fan, based on their fans!

Our analysis has found no reasons to be a fan, based on their fans!

8 CITY

Our analysis has found no reasons to be a fan, based on their city!

Our analysis has found no reasons to be a fan, based on their city!

Our analysis has found no reasons to be a fan, based on their city!

Our analysis has found no reasons to be a fan, based on their city!

9 MASCOT

Our analysis has found no reasons to be a fan, based on their mascot!

Our analysis has found no reasons to be a fan, based on their mascot!

Our analysis has found no reasons to be a fan, based on their mascot!

Our analysis has found no reasons to be a fan, based on their mascot!

Our analysis has found no reasons to be a fan, based on their mascot!

Our analysis has found no reasons to be a fan, based on their mascot!

Our analysis has found no reasons to be a fan, based on their mascot!

Our analysis has found no reasons to be a fan, based on their mascot!

Our analysis has found no reasons to be a fan, based on their mascot!

10 SPONSORS

Our analysis has found no reasons to be a fan, based on their sponsors!

Our analysis has found no reasons to be a fan, based on their sponsors!

Our analysis has found no reasons to be a fan, based on their sponsors!

Our analysis has found no reasons to be a fan, based on their sponsors!

ABOUT THE AUTHOR

Max Hater holds a B.S. (the alternative B.S. to a Bachelor of Science) in Hater and Fan Analysis. Hater has accumulated years of thorough research and analysis of these fans and haters. His unique work provides an understanding of the theories of fan and hater behavior regarding a broad range of topics, as well as analysis of the empirical research on the emotions, thoughts, and behaviors of these fans and haters. Using a multidisciplinary approach, a variety of fascinating topics such as identification, worship, and motivation have been identified and examined. This book provides an understanding of the importance of these fans and haters and provides an intelligent guide for following the same motives to become the best fan and/or hater possible.

Find Max on Twitter: @MaxHater1
Find Max on Facebook: @MaxHater1
Find Max on Instagram: @MaxHater

www.MaxHater.com

Made in the USA
Coppell, TX
10 December 2019

WITH THE WORD

A BIBLE STUDY AND DEVOTIONAL GUIDE
FOR GROUPS OR INDIVIDUALS

MennoMedia

Harrisonburg, VA
Waterloo, ON

With the Word: Acts
Copyright © 2013 by MennoMedia, Harrisonburg, Virginia 22802
    Released simultaneously in Canada by MennoMedia,
    Waterloo, Ontario N2L 6H7. All rights reserved.
International Standard Book Number: 978-0-8361-9694-8
Printed in United States of America
Edited by Linda Gehman Peachey, cover and interior design by Merrill R. Miller

Sessions from *Adult Bible Study Teacher* and *Adult Bible Study Student*, along with
Rejoice! daily devotions, were all used in the writing of *With the Word: Acts*.

To order or request information, please call 1-800-245-7894 in the U.S.
or 1-800-631-6535 in Canada. Or visit www.mennomedia.org.

16 15 14 13   10 9 8 7 6 5 4 3 2 1

Table of contents

Introduction

* *

Welcome to *With the Word*! This exciting series from MennoMedia invites you to draw closer to God by spending time with the Word through Bible study and daily devotions.

Studying Acts

When we start reading Acts, we soon discover that it is a continuation of Luke. Acts is dedicated to the same person, refers back to the third gospel, briefly overlaps with it, and then carries its story forward. We further note that the style is like that of Luke and its interests are similar.

Acts is thus a *continuing gospel*, a proclamation of the good news of Jesus Christ that is carried on by a Holy Spirit–empowered church.

This way of composing the book has suggested a title such as "The Acts of Peter and Paul." In view of the commissioning in 1:8, a better name might be "The Acts of the Holy Spirit," or perhaps "The Spirit-Directed Witness from Jerusalem to Rome." The present title, "The Acts of the Apostles," was attached to the work about the middle of the second century. It no doubt reflects the mention of the apostles as a group through the first 15 chapters and the fact that Paul is cast in that role for the remainder of the book.

Permeating all these interests and tying them together is the most basic one of them all: the divine guidance and empowerment provided by the Holy Spirit, with the accompaniment of prayer, signs, wonders, visions, angels, and prophetic utterances. God is at work on every page! To list examples and give references would result in a topical index of almost every paragraph in Acts. This is so central that there are more words for power in the book than there are for love. Concern and compassion are not lacking. Indeed, they are implied in every aspect of the gospel message. But the "acts" needed to witness to the ends of the earth are primarily manifestations of power, meetings and conquering the authority structures of the pagan world.

The missionary method found in Acts is that of (1) basic preaching and teaching, (2) accompanied by signs and wonders. Again and again people can see the gospel, the inbreaking of the new order (by miracles), as well as hear it (in spoken messages). This gives the Christian evangelists two mutual reinforcing forms of witness with which to carry the message from Jerusalem to Rome.

—from Chalmer E. Faw, *Acts*, Believers Church Bible Commentary (Scottdale, PA: Herald Press, 1993), 17–18, 25. Used by permission.

Session format

. . . .

In this volume on Acts, you will find eight sessions for either group or individual use. The easy-to-use format starts with an in-depth Bible study and ends with seven short devotionals designed to be read in the days after the session. Here's a guide to each session:

- **Opening:** The opening of the Bible-study portion calls you into the session through a summary of the text and a few questions for reflection. Before you begin each session, take time to read the text reflectively.

- **For the leader:** These are ideas for how to use the material in a group setting. If using the material individually, omit this section.

- **Understanding God's Word:** This section makes connections between the session's text and today's world.

- **Connecting with God's Word:** This is the heart of the guide; it's the in-depth Bible study that calls you to examine specific parts of the session's text. The writer gives background for a few verses of text, then outlines a series of questions for personal reflection or discussion. These questions always invite you to make connections between the biblical text and your own life.

- **Closing:** The Bible-study portion of the session then closes with a brief time of worship and wrapping up.

- **Devotionals:** Immediately after the sessions you will find seven short devotionals on the session's text. Each devotional starts with a Scripture verse, includes a meditation, and ends with a prayer. Use these seven inspiring devotionals in the days after the session as way to keep the text in your heart and mind.

Spend time *With the Word* today!

Encountering the Spirit

Acts 2:1-12

* *

Opening

Think about times in your life when you have been especially energized and transformed by the Holy Spirit. Also, when have you observed God's Spirit at work in a group or church in an unusually powerful way? What elements are common to such experiences? What characteristics indicate that God's Spirit is at work?

Understanding God's Word

Luke begins the dramatic story of Acts with the risen Jesus telling his followers to wait. God has promised that Jesus will continue to be present and active on earth through the new spiritual body God is creating. Believers will become Christ's witnesses through power from God. The Holy Spirit comes to this group as they wait for God to act.

It is significant that this occurs at Pentecost. Taken from the Greek word for 50, this festival is observed seven weeks, or 50 days, after Passover. It marks the end of the wheat harvest and the giving of the Law to God's people on Mount Sinai. Devout pilgrims, from all the lands to which Jews have

* *

For the leader

1. Briefly review what Jesus' followers have experienced in the preceding weeks: Jesus' triumphal entry, his arrest and crucifixion, and then Jesus' amazing resurrection, surprising appearances, and ascension into heaven. Now these followers are meeting and praying together, waiting as Jesus has instructed them, for guidance and power from God for the future.

2. Ask four people to read these verses in turn: Acts 2:1-4, 5-8, 9-11, 12-13. What words or images stand out and grab your attention?

emigrated, have returned to Jerusalem to celebrate their national history and identity.

Just as God's Spirit has anointed Jesus for ministry at his baptism (Luke 3:22) and in his first sermon (Luke 4:14-19), the Holy Spirit now fills the believers with Christ's living presence. Jesus' earthly mission is over, but his new body—the church—is born. And Jesus' mission on earth will continue.

Connecting with God's Word

A new creation

The 120 waiting believers heard a sound like that of a tornado filling their building. God's *Ruakh* (wind, spirit) had arrived with awesome power. God's *Ruakh* was the creative power that had brought the world and humanity into being (Genesis 1–2). It was the wind that had dried up the Red Sea for the Israelites to cross in safety so that they could become a covenant community (Exodus 14).

The tongues of fire call to mind the pillar of fire by which God led his people in the wilderness and showed God's special presence. Other associations between fire and the divine presence can be found in Exodus 3:2-4, where the angel of the Lord appears to Moses in a "flame of fire" out of a bush, and in Exodus 19:18, where God descends onto Mount Sinai in fire.

At Pentecost, Spirit fire appeared and settled on each individual's head. Jeremiah's prophecy that God's Word would dwell in each person's heart was being fulfilled (Jeremiah 31:31-34). Each believer received a new spiritual identity and a place in the Christian community.

Wind and fire are symbols of creation and of God's presence with people. In Genesis they symbolize the creation of family, and in Exodus, the creation of the children of Israel. Here they signal the creation of a new community, representing reconciliation between God and humanity and with one another. The church was a new family, defined and shaped by the character, life, and teachings of Jesus.

- What makes the church different from other associations of people? How is the Holy Spirit active in the church in a unique way?

- What are the primary characteristics of a Spirit-filled life? See 1 Corinthians 13:1-7 and Galatians 5:22-23.

- Explore your hymnbook for songs that describe the character and work of the Holy Spirit or that pray for spiritual revival. What do you learn from those perspectives?

A worldwide community

Luke lists 15 regions from which the gathered onlookers came. They were all able to understand what the enthusiastic believers were saying about God's wonderful works. This miracle of hearing one's native language was a reversal of Babel. Whereas God "confused" humans by dividing them into different languages when they sought to become like God, here we see the beginning of a great reversal of that division. At Pentecost, language and cultural differences were broken down—embraced and redeemed in the church.

These pilgrims were not literally "from every nation under heaven," but Luke uses their diversity to show that the gospel is intended for all people everywhere. The places listed are similar to those found in other ancient descriptions spanning the "known world" of that day. These people took the gospel home with them when they left Jerusalem. From its very beginning, God's intention was for the church to be universal and inclusive in its nature and mission.

Pentecost was an evangelistic event that set into motion the global reach of the gospel. Communication was key. The disciples came out of seclusion and spoke in Spirit-given languages. All spoke intelligibly in languages not their own. The Spirit's gift is not confusing sounds, but fluent and understandable speech. Speaking in many languages remains necessary for Christ's work to continue today.

Powerful awakenings have occurred throughout history. Individuals, churches, and Christian institutions frequently need an updating of the Spirit's presence. The results include dynamic changes in people's lives, reconciliation, renewed love and vision for the church, and zeal for communicating the gospel.

- Do you know languages other than your native one? How has this shaped your worldview or changed your relationships with people?

- How does God's Spirit enlarge the community and break down barriers caused by different languages, cultures, and perspectives? How is our understanding of God enlarged by incorporating new languages and cultures into the church?

- What events or experiences draw people in your church together and promote understanding?

Closing

Sing or read the hymn "Holy Spirit, Come with Power" (number 26 in *Hymnal: A Worship Book* [Scottdale, PA: Mennonite Publishing House, 1992]) or another hymn about the Holy Spirit.

DEVOTIONALS

* *

Devotional 1

Suddenly from heaven there came a sound like the rush of a violent wind, and it filled the entire house where they were sitting.
—Acts 2:2

I am amazed at the power of the wind. When vacationing on Prince Edward Island, we learned about wind as a great source of energy.

In a similar way, the Spirit of Pentecost is a creative force that gives life and faith. When we are filled with God's Spirit, we become a creative, powerful source of energy. We use the unique abilities that God's Spirit has entrusted to each of us. When we use our gifts, we see a little of God's creative Spirit at work in our world.

Just as the disciples, we are given power and boldness to continue the work of Jesus. God's Spirit energizes us to share the good news of God's kingdom with others. Like a gale of wind, God's Spirit will do amazing things in our lives. Let's open the windows of our house and welcome the strong wind of God's Spirit. *–Sandi Hannigan Marr*

Spirit of God, come upon me like a mighty gale of wind. Help me use my gifts to serve others and share your good news with boldness and courage.

Devotional 2

Suddenly from heaven there came a sound like the rush of a violent wind, and it filled the entire house where they were sitting.
—Acts 2:2

How do we sense the movement of the Holy Spirit? Some think of receiving spiritual gifts such as speaking in tongues, healing, and prophecy. Others experience God pushing them to risk encountering a new situation that feels strange and intimidating.

Our church has been helping people discern their spiritual gifts, challenging them to ask, "What do I have a passion for? What am I good at? How can I turn those interests and abilities into a ministry God can use?" At Pentecost the believers spoke in new languages, and we too are learning that God's creative Spirit often stretches us beyond what we think we can do.

Often the Spirit's movement is manifested in unstructured ways. For instance, a group of retired women prays weekly about concerns in our church. Others provide much-needed comfort food for those who are sick or hurting. The possibilities are endless. *–Ann Minter Fetters*

God, may the wind of your Spirit blow freely in my life today. Move me to take up your work with energy and freedom.

* * * * * * * * * * * * * * *

Devotional 3

All of [the disciples] were filled with the Holy Spirit and began to speak in other languages, as the Spirit gave them ability. —Acts 2:4

Recently I was talking about an insight I had, and I used the phrase *It hit me*. Three-year-old Isaiah looked at me, puzzled, and asked, "What hit you, Miss Karen?" I tried to explain, but he continued to look puzzled.

I think of that incident when reading this passage from Acts. Usually we try to make our meanings clear to others, taking into account their point of view, experience, and age. In this story, the Spirit made the message clear to everyone.

We can ask God for wisdom when we speak to others, trusting the Spirit will give the right words. Even so, there are times when the message may not be understood right away, and we can leave the outcome in God's hands. Isaiah's ability to understand will deepen and mature. I hope that I also will continue to grow in my understanding of God and in my ability to communicate clearly. *—Karen Jantzi*

God, give me words to help people understand your message of grace and love. Grant me patience to wait for growth in both myself and others.

* * * * * * * * * * * * * * *

Devotional 4

The crowd . . . was bewildered, because each one heard them speaking in the native language of each. —Acts 2:6

In the beginning the world had one language and a common speech (Genesis 11:1-8). The people wanted to build a tower to the heavens to make themselves the center of the world, but God "scattered them . . . over the face of all the earth" by confusing their language.

At Pentecost, the event that birthed the Christian church (Acts 2), the disciples were filled with the Holy Spirit and spoke in other languages so all could understand in their own dialects.

In the Genesis story, the people try to make their own way to heaven. They do not listen to God but want to do things their own way. In Acts 2 the people are listening and asking questions. They want to hear the Word and each other. And so God gathers them together to learn about God's deeds and God's power. Babel separates; Pentecost brings together. *—Bernie Wiebe*

Thank you, Holy Spirit, for gathering your people in all the earth. Help us learn to listen to you and to each other.

* * * * * * * * * * * * * * *

Devotional 5

In our own languages we hear them speaking about God's deeds of power. —Acts 2:11b

In my home community of Clovis, California, the desire to create relationships with other believers has begun taking root. One Sunday our sisters and brothers from Iglesia el Buen Pastor joined our congregation for worship and a fund-raising fellowship meal. The proceeds of the meal would help their youth travel to Mexico to learn about their heritage of culture and faith.

Despite the language barrier, we sang each other's songs, read Scriptures in both Spanish and English, and listened to a gifted speaker who used both languages. An older woman shared how she felt God's love during a retreat of both groups as the women sewed together and shared baby-tending duties.

As we enjoyed delicious tacos, salsa, and flan, we lingered with our new friends. Their generous serving and cheerful sharing of cleanup chores in a very hot kitchen became signs of the way Pentecost continues in the church today. —*Nancy Becker*

Dear God, help me learn to know others in your community of faith who, though they may not speak my native language, can teach me the power of your Spirit.

* * * * * * * * * * * * * * * *
Devotional 6

We hear them declaring the wonders of God in our own tongues! —Acts 1:11b (NIV)

I was once at a workshop where we tried to identify each other's personality types. Even for those of us who didn't know the lingo, the exercise became a celebration of the variety of strengths and quirks God has given us humans.

Each of us has our unique way of understanding, interpreting, and talking about the world and God. The wonder of Pentecost was that each person in the crowd heard God's message in his or her own dialect. I'm sure that understanding went deeper than words. This gospel spoke to the inner language of personality and worldview, at the level of understanding and experience of each listener.

What dawned at Pentecost was faith in a God who not only enters human experience through Jesus, but whose Spirit envelops and fills any personality, from any culture. This God gets to the core of who I am and speaks my language.
—*Byron Rempel-Burkholder*

God, if anyone understands me to my core, it is you. Grant me ears to hear you speaking my language, and courage to respond.

* * * * * * * * * * * * * * * *
Devotional 7

All were amazed and perplexed, saying to one another, "What does this mean?"
—Acts 2:12

"I see it but can hardly believe it" is a comment we make when reality doesn't match our expectations. Maybe a child excels or falls short of what we expect. Or a new job opportunity far exceeds our dreams. Maybe our relationship with God isn't bringing the results we anticipate.

I imagine that the faithful Jews celebrating Pentecost in Jerusalem thought they knew how events would unroll. The festival had been held for centuries; why should this year have been different from others? No wonder they experienced so much bewilderment, amazement, and astonishment at what they saw and heard.

Is it possible our gatherings for worship become humdrum because we assume we know what will happen? Is our personal life in Christ less than what God intends because we don't expect much? What God has in mind may be a wonderful demonstration of power—even if we don't expect it.
—*Nadine Friesen*

God of surprises and power, keep me alert to the wonderful demonstrations of your power and goodness.

Repent and be baptized

Acts 2:12-42

* *

Opening

Today's session focuses on new experiences and information which force people to rethink what they know about God and God's will. Recall an experience which led you to reevaluate what you thought you knew about God and faithfulness. Who helped you in this process? What sermons, books, or other resources helped you gain new understanding and integrate the experience into your faith journey? How did this help you move in a new direction or onto a more faithful path?

Understanding God's Word

It is helpful to remember again all that has happened in Jerusalem over the preceding weeks. Jesus' death and resurrection have been difficult for even the disciples to absorb and understand. No one expected that the Messiah would be crucified. He was to be their Savior, so it seemed impossible that he would be killed! And can someone really rise from the dead?

Certainly Jesus has given them much insight and understanding before ascending to heaven. Yet as they wait for further guidance, the disciples no doubt continue to reflect, pray, and search the Scriptures in order to better

* *

For the leader

1. This is a long passage—including some narration, Peter's sermon, a quote from Joel, and several quotes from Psalms. Ask someone to play the part of the narrator, another to be Peter, and two others to read the verses from Joel (Acts 2:17-21) and David (Acts 2:25b-28, 31b, 34b-35).

2. Share your reflections from the opening exercise, or invite someone else in the group to share about an experience of repentance and change. This can be from when they were baptized or a later time when they realized that something in their life needed to change.

Acts 2:12-42

understand and integrate this into their faith journey.

Amazingly, Peter is the one able to draw on Scripture to explain these remarkable events to the crowds. He has been a cowardly betrayer of Jesus, but now he becomes a courageous witness and an insightful interpreter of Scripture.

Connecting with God's Word

New understanding

Certainly, what happened at Pentecost was truly surprising. Here were these unsophisticated Galileans speaking in many languages! How could this be? No wonder some reacted with scornful put-downs, labeling the speakers as drunken idiots.

But Peter did not respond in kind. Rather, he drew from within their Jewish heritage in order to help explain what was taking place. First, the language miracle was the fulfillment of Joel's prophecy (Joel 2:28-32). God was giving the gift of the Spirit to both genders, to all ages and economic classes. Each individual had new intimacy with God that gave them confidence to speak God's message.

Then Peter explained that although Jesus' deeds had pointed people to God, they had violently rejected Jesus and his message. God, however, had raised Jesus from the dead and exalted him. This crucified and risen Jesus was their Lord and Messiah. To back this up, Peter again quoted Scripture to show that the Messiah would be resurrected and made Lord of all.

Interestingly, this sermon and the many others recorded by Luke show the importance of the spoken word in the church. While the loud wind, tongues of fire, and many voices drew attention to the Spirit's work, it took words of explanation to help people make sense of what they saw and heard.

- Sermons and the spoken word continue to be important in most worship services. What has this meant in your life? What types of messages are especially compelling or convincing? To what extent do you appreciate connecting with past traditions? When is a totally new insight or interpretation helpful?

- Many of the onlookers were tempted to dismiss the disciples as "Galileans," people not expected to be educated or able to speak multiple languages. When have you learned something from an unexpected source?

- Why might those on the margins be able to perceive something new or have a perspective different from those who are more at the center of power and society?

Repent and be baptized

Peter's blunt words, "You crucified your Messiah," elicited deep sorrow in the guilty crowd. They pled with the apostles for guidance, so Peter responded with clear instructions.

Repentance is God's gift enabling people to turn and change their understanding and actions. Baptism means joining Jesus' new body in a public act that identifies an individual with Jesus the Messiah. As new converts become part of the community, they find reconciliation with God and with others. The gift of God's Spirit and new life extended to all people in Peter's time, and it extends to everyone in our time and into the future. Peter's final advice was that they must let themselves be saved. Salvation won't come through allegiance to old ways or former religious or national identity.

Salvation comes through Jesus Christ and is lived in the faith community. Incredibly, three thousand people grasped the significance of Peter's encouraging message, received forgiveness, and moved into a new life in the new community.

To show that this wasn't simply a short-term spiritual high, Luke lists four ongoing activities of the new community. The converts needed to learn more of Jesus' message and how to be faithful to him, so the apostles, who had accompanied Jesus, became teachers. The fellowship of this large group wasn't based on old friendships but on their new bonds of love for the Lord and concern for each other. The "breaking of bread" reinforced their sense of Jesus' presence. It reminded them of Jesus' miracles of feeding thousands of people and his postresurrection appearance in Emmaus (Luke 24:28-35). "The prayers" brought them together in the temple to worship God.

- What does repentance mean? How has this been part of your life? Is it a one-time event or something ongoing?

- How do you understand baptism? Read some worship resources: numbers 775–779 in *Hymnal: A Worship Book* or numbers 166–168 in *Sing the Journey* (Scottdale, PA: Mennonite Publishing Network, 2005). What images and concepts are especially meaningful? How would you explain this to a new believer?

Closing

Sing or read together "New Earth, Heavens New" (number 299 in *Hymnal: A Worship Book*), "I Sought the Lord" (number 506 in *Hymnal: A Worship Book*), or "Like a Tender Breath, Stirring" (number 106 in *Sing the Story* [Scottdale, PA: Mennonite Publishing Network, 2007]).

DEVOTIONALS

* *

Devotional 1

In the last days, God says, I will pour out my Spirit on all people. —Acts 2:17a (NIV)

It is hard to imagine what Pentecost was like, but strange things were clearly happening. People heard sounds like a tornado, saw tongues of fire, and heard people speaking in strange languages.

Peter explains that this is what the prophet Joel foresaw: an outpouring of the Spirit upon all humanity, not just Hebrews. Sons and daughters, men and women, old and young, and even servants would prophesy.

This is still a sign of the Spirit moving among us. Our hearts should be full of fear and trembling if our sons and daughters have no godly visions or the dreamers do not include older adults. Our hearts should ache if the voice of prophets has dwindled to a pip-squeak. To shut down the Spirit's working limits God. To observe Pentecost and the coming of the Holy Spirit opens us to its freedom as we work in partnership with God. *—Katie Funk Wiebe*

Renew your church, O God; restore its ministries through the empowerment of your Spirit. May prophets, dreamers, and visionaries speak boldly your hope for the world.

Devotional 2

Your sons and your daughters will prophesy. —Acts 2:17.

My 93-year-old mother saw the advent of the modern age. The clip-clop of horse and wagon gave way to the jet's roar in her lifetime. My childhood on the farm flowed into middle-aged wrestling with computer viruses.

Each of us has to work out our salvation in the context of our own generation. We find new music that helps us worship, and we coin new vocabulary to express our faith. While we may not view each other as "drunk," we still question whether the Holy Spirit could possibly be present in another generation's puzzling behavior.

Peter quotes the prophet Joel to assure us that the Holy Spirit is not limited by history. In the midst of what feels like fear and chaos, God's Spirit will continue to pour through our sons and daughters, and through strangers who speak other languages. God's Spirit will still be there, transforming people and the future world. *—Mary Lou Cummings*

O God, give me Peter's confidence. Fill me with hope and trust for the future. Open my heart to the Holy Spirit moving in new ways in each generation.

* * * * * * * * * * * * * * *

Devotional 3

Your sons and your daughters shall prophesy, and your young men shall see visions, and your old men shall dream dreams.
—Acts 2:17

In this sermon Peter quotes the prophet Joel to explain the coming of the Holy Spirit among the apostles. We may think this doesn't happen today. Yet if we are open, we do see God continuing to work out visions and dreams in tangible ways. Not only can we find fulfillment in our own souls but we can also let God use us to fulfill God's plans for the world around us.

When my father retired, he knew he wasn't done with God's work. He saw a need in his community for a kid-friendly place where youth could learn and play, mentored by staff who valued them as individuals. He envisioned a gym, a recreation room, tutoring facilities, a computer lab, and a woodworking shop.

Many said it couldn't be done, but there now stands a beautiful facility where children's laughter fills the air. The Spirit was leading my father in his dreams. How will the Spirit lead you today?
–Ann Minter Fetters

God, grant me visions and dreams today. Show me concrete ways that I can be a channel for your Spirit.

* * * * * * * * * * * * * * *

Devotional 4

Even on my servants, both men and women, I will pour out my Spirit in those days, and they will prophesy. —Acts 2:18 (NIV)

One of the fascinating trends in the global church is the shifting of its center of gravity from North to South. Since the late '90s, for example, there have been more Mennonites in Africa, Asia, and Latin America than in Europe and North America. One thing this shift means for us in Canada and the United States is that we now take our turn at being on the fringes, with less influence on the global church than we had at one time.

I wonder if Peter's sermon was preserved for the benefit of Jewish Christians in the early church who worried about the shift of the church's center away from Jerusalem. The Spirit was no longer the privilege of a few Israelite servants of God. But they were still included! Even though we may feel sidelined, when the Spirit moves, no one is left on the fringes.
–Byron Rempel-Burkholder

God, your Spirit knows no bounds. May my true center today be the place where love and grace reach.

* * * * * * * * * * * * * * *

Devotional 5

Repent, and be baptized every one of you in the name of Jesus Christ . . . and you will receive the gift of the Holy Spirit. —Acts 2:38

I don't remember what drew Joe to our church. He had no personal or family connections. He was alone in the world and searching for meaning. He heard the gospel and saw our attempts to live it. He soon began asking how to become part of the church. When he heard Acts 2:38, it sounded too good to be true. But Joe was ready for new life in Christ.

Countless people have followed these steps—repentance, baptism, and receiving of the Holy Spirit—which open the door to the boundless possibilities available through Jesus' resurrection. We begin this journey

Acts 2:12-42

of faith and are continually renewed within the believing community. The rest of Acts 2 describes the rich life of the early believers, who bonded together, worshiped together, and proclaimed the Word fearlessly. It is a preview of the world-changing ministry they were given, and in which we share.
—Keith Harder

God, give me a glimpse of the possibilities that await me through repentance, baptism, and receiving the Holy Spirit.

* * * * * * * * * * * * * *

Devotional 6

The promise is for you, for your children, and for all who are far away, everyone whom the Lord our God calls. —Acts 2:39

What dreadful scenarios give you chills in the middle of the night? Sharks? Mad cow disease? Snakes? Falling out a window to cement below?

Strangely, most of us worry about the wrong things. We spend lots of mental energy trying to make our lives happy and safe, but we often avoid the most important questions and put off changing the behaviors that put us most at risk.

Here Peter tries to communicate what is most urgent and essential. He implores the crowd: "Receive God's forgiveness for your sins. Receive the gift of the Holy Spirit. You and your children can save yourselves!"

All of us crave security and peace, longing for confidence in the truth at the core of our existence. Paul tells us that our culture won't give it to us. Our worries won't save us. But if we are willing to receive the gift of salvation, it is waiting for us.
—Mary Lou Cummings

Savior God, I give my worries for you to hold, so that my hands can be free to accept the gifts of love you shower on me.

* * * * * * * * * * * * * *

Devotional 7

So those who welcomed his message were baptized. . . . They devoted themselves to the apostles' teaching and fellowship, to the breaking of bread and the prayers.
—Acts 2:41-42

Recently I watched a teenager fall in love with physics. "Physics is simply playing with toys," the teacher said. Start with three balls and bounce each separately. Each bounces about the same. Stacked, however, the lower balls transfer momentum to the upper one, greatly increasing the height of the bounce.

So can't you hear the buzz at that first Pentecost when people realize they understand the person next to them? Can't you imagine the transfer of energy as they realize it isn't happening just to them but to everyone? It must have been like people transferring momentum to each other.

It was the momentum they needed to move along the difficult, rewarding path that their love for Jesus set before them. They discovered that working together produced more than the simple sum of the parts.

We also need this transfer of momentum for spiritual health. This is a physics of the Spirit. Can't you feel the bounce?
—Lani Wright

May we be open to your Spirit and your energy as we grow in our love for you and learn to be your people.

3

Sharing community

Acts 2:37-47; 4:32-35

* *

Opening

These passages are full of drama and enthusiasm. As you read them, reflect on how you imagine the events. What colors, sounds, and emotions are present? If you painted the scenes or wrote a play, what would you highlight? What is most attractive? What is disturbing or makes you hesitate? Where are people today experiencing something similar to this kind of renewal and community life?

Understanding God's Word

Luke uses brief summaries to end various sections in his account, such as those in today's lesson and in Acts 6:7; 9:31; 12:24; 16:5; 19:20; and 28:31. Each summary highlights the growth of the church.

Clearly, the whole community benefits from the breaking down of economic and social barriers and the growing unity among the believers. Their gratitude to God for new life shows in all their relationships. The mutual love within the church attracts many to this Spirit-filled community.

* *

For the leader

1. Read this passage in three sections: Acts 2:37-42; 2:43-47; 4:32-35. Invite people to share the one word that came to mind as they heard these verses.

2. Many Western Christians assume this type of sharing was short lived, yet mutual aid and caring for the poor continued to be central practices of the early Christian church. It was also practiced among the Anabaptists and in other renewal movements, such as Catholic Worker communities in the United States and base Christian communities in Latin America. As you wrestle with this challenge in your context, encourage the group to be creative and bold in thinking about specific steps they can take, and what blessings might await them.

20   *Acts 2:37-47; 4:32-35*

Connecting with God's Word

All things in common

Members of the new community were together, and they became united in their attitudes and actions. From self-serving individuals they were transformed into a loving fellowship by Christ's Spirit. That same Spirit gave them the motivation to put themselves and their resources completely into Christ's service.

Having goods in common showed that something hugely significant had happened. The believers were set free from a tight grip on their wallets and personal property. Instead, they searched for ways they could use their money to express gratitude to God and love for their neighbor. Kindness was considered the ideal of true friendship in Greek culture. But giving to needy people with such generosity and joy went far beyond the norm.

We don't know if this giving was an expectation for all. We don't know if those helped were limited to the faith community or included others in the neighborhood. What we do know is that poverty and economic oppression were widespread. Luke makes it clear that common ownership and Christlike sharing are miracles that demonstrate the power of God's Spirit. These activities are an impressive witness to the world.

Homes also became intimate settings for worship and fellowship. As the new Christians opened their homes for daily love feasts, eating together was more than filling empty stomachs or just socializing. The meals fostered greater love, unity, and openness among them. They were evidence of a new spirit of hospitality and generosity. Breaking bread was a memorial of the last supper with Jesus. It was also a celebration of his continuing presence and a foretaste of the heavenly kingdom banquet to come.

Over the centuries, Christians have attempted to copy the communal life of the early church. Catholic monastic traditions and Hutterite colonies come to mind. Richard Foster, in *Freedom of Simplicity*, states that we are not to slavishly imitate what occurred in the early days of the church. Instead, we need to see their "incredible freedom to experiment with practical ways to flesh out the meaning of love for God and neighbor. Under the authority of Christ, they were freed to try new ways to love one another" (p. 55).

- How do you build togetherness, compassion, and trust within your local congregation? What new ways of loving and caring could your congregation try?

- *Community*, *communion*, and *communication* all have the same Latin root, *communis*, which means "to hold in common." How do these three interrelate in your life? How do shared meals and communion services reflect the Spirit's presence for you?

Not a needy person among them

In his second summary (4:32-35), Luke again reports that the believers were united and held all things in common. This was not superficial unity nor forced generosity. God's great power was visible in the apostles' teaching and miracles and in prayers that were answered. Divine power dramatically transformed and guided all their economic decisions.

The early church was fulfilling the Scriptures that prophesied there would be no needy people among the Israelites if they obeyed God's will (Deuteronomy 15:4-5). Their compassion glorified God and showed what kind of world God wants for all people.

Selling property to release money for humanitarian work was exactly what Jesus had told the rich young ruler to do: "Sell all that you own and distribute the money to the poor, and you will have treasure in heaven" (Luke 18:22). The believers were wholeheartedly obeying Jesus' teaching about showing mercy and bringing good news to the poor. The mundane affairs of buying and selling and handling money were linked to the transforming work of the risen Lord.

Sharing our wealth is a spiritual matter. Money can tempt us to greed, corruption, and abuse. God is glorified, however, if we view all our resources as sacred, and if we use and share them to confront and alleviate poverty, injustice, and inequality.

- The early church did not treat money as a private issue. In that spirit, talk with someone about how you use money to honor God. What economic sharing have you done? What are your financial temptations? How do you experience God's Spirit in relation to your finances?

- Read through the hymn "Take My Life" (number 389 in *Hymnal: A Worship Book*). Which aspects of your life are easiest to yield to God? Which are most difficult?

Closing

Sing the hymn "Take My Life," number 389, or pray the offering prayer, number 750, both in *Hymnal: A Worship Book*.

Acts 2:37-47; 4:32-35

DEVOTIONALS

Devotional 1

Now when they heard this, they were cut to the heart and said to Peter and to the other apostles, "Brothers, what should we do?"
—Acts 2:37

Who we are as Christ's followers is important, but not to the exclusion of doing. Following Peter's statement that we can "know with certainty" (2:36) that Jesus is Lord and Messiah, those present asked, "What should we do?" Peter's declaration of Jesus' identity called for a response on the part of those who chose to follow him.

His answer includes many "doing" words: repent and be baptized, devote yourselves to teaching and fellowship, participate in communion and prayer. The doing, in turn, affects our understanding of who we are. We are people called to life with Christ and to separation from corruption. We are part of a community that has heard and welcomed his message.

Take a moment today to review what we do as Jesus' disciples and to celebrate who we are in Christ. It's important to do what we are and to be what we do.
–Nadine Friesen

Forgive me, Lord, for the times when I try to choose between being and doing. I receive both my identity and my ability to live in obedience as your gifts of grace.

Devotional 2

For the promise is for you, for your children, and for all who are far away, everyone whom the Lord our God calls to him.
—Acts 2:39

To visit the Balcony House ruins at Mesa Verde National Park, Colorado, you must descend the sheer side of a cliff on a stairwell, then climb a broad ladder. The ruins were probably a center for religious ceremonies.

Hiking this ruin is physically demanding. You have to walk through tight corridors, then get down on your hands and knees to exit through a small tunnel. The tunnel symbolized a birth canal. It reminded people they needed to be born again and again, each time they worshiped.

The symbolism may reflect the universal call of the gospel and the need for all to be "born again." Although the Ancestral Pueblo peoples did not live in a time and place in which to hear the story of Jesus, they were granted some insight into God's plan for their lives. Surely, all these peoples were part of the promise that Peter proclaimed at Pentecost. *–Frank Ramirez*

God, you have given us a story to tell to the nations. Help us to see and hear how that story crosses all barriers, calling all people to you.

* * * * * * * * * * * * * *

Devotional 3

Those who welcomed his message were baptized, and that day about three thousand persons were added. —Acts 2:41

My father was a pastor and evangelist who often visited people in their homes. One day he sensed God telling him to turn into a farmyard. To his shock he discovered the farmer in the barn, trying to hang himself from one of the beams. By God's grace my father was able to talk him into coming down. He then led him to accept Jesus Christ, helping him find grace and salvation.

On the day of Pentecost, when Peter explained what had happened to Jesus, the people were "cut to the heart." Peter invited them to repentance and baptism, and many responded.

How ready are we to take up Jesus' call to "go into all the world" with the good news? The Bible is clear that this task belongs to us. As we go into the world today, let us be prepared to share the good news with conviction. *–David Wiebe*

God, please help me to spread the message of your grace and kingdom. Bring people into my life who will enable me to do so. Thank you for leading me.

* * * * * * * * * * * * * *

Devotional 4

They devoted themselves to the apostles' teaching and fellowship, to the breaking of bread and the prayers. —Acts 2:42

When my sister lived in the deep woods of northern Wisconsin, she would rise daily and train for her cross-country ski races. She would head out into the bitter winter dawn,

whooshing through the snow in silence, building up speed, muscle, and strength—her mind on the competition to come.

In the same way, we condition ourselves to live the Christian life. Those who were baptized following Peter's sermon studied the gospel, sought fellowship with other believers, broke bread together, and continued in regular prayer. In practicing these disciplines, they were preparing for the journey ahead.

Just as my sister trained herself by facing the bitter cold, snow, and ice, so we need to practice habits that will see us through our own spiritual journey. In your time of reflection, evaluate the habits you have or would like to cultivate, habits to help you face the challenges lying ahead. *–Ann Minter Fetters*

Help me to grow my faith by practicing habits that will make me stronger. In those disciplines may I find joy.

* * * * * * * * * * * * * *

Devotional 5

They devoted themselves to the apostles' teaching and fellowship, to the breaking of bread and the prayers. —Acts 2:42

Sun. Rain. Soil. These are individual elements of nature. Each is completely distinct from the others. But when we observe how they cooperate with one another, we have a picture of the fellowship that God intends for Christians to experience.

Imagine a world where the elements of nature exist in separate compartments. It would be ridiculous. The world that God created is interactive! The elements function together to produce the beauty of nature we all enjoy.

Acts 2:37-47; 4:32-35

What about our lives as Christians? Do we compartmentalize the elements listed here? Biblical teaching, fellowship, eating, prayer—these are not designed to exist in isolation. As these early Christians were involved in one another's lives, the results listed in verses 43-47 were amazing. Just as soil, sun, and rain function together to produce new plant life, so Christians living in close fellowship produce an environment that fosters the birth of new believers. —Nancy Heidebrecht Kelley

God, help me understand the importance of involvement in the lives of other believers. Lead me to true fellowship so that others may find life in you.

* * * * * * * * * * * * * * *

Devotional 6

They devoted themselves to the apostles' teaching and fellowship, to the breaking of bread and the prayers. —Acts 2:42

During the 1980s we were listed in the *Mennonite Your Way Directory*, a denominational hospitality directory. The world came alive for our children. All visits included time at the table, sharing plentiful meals. Regardless of barriers of language, race, and cultural assumptions, we could always break bread together.

The Roman Empire, which provided a crucible for the Christian experiment, divided people into categories. Slave and free, men and women, rich and poor, Jew and Gentile, noble and commoner, day laborer and craftsperson—all were separated by barriers that prevented them from eating together.

Christians defied these social taboos and met together at one table, sharing the staff of life as taught by the God of life. It was an audacious practice that our modern churches—too often separated by race, economics, and language—sometimes fail to practice. Jesus calls us to one table. We are the body. He is the Bread. —*Frank Ramirez*

God, help us break down barriers that exist in our churches, whether of wealth, culture, language, ability, or age. We desire to fellowship with all.

* * * * * * * * * * * * * * *

Devotional 7

They broke bread at home and ate their food with glad and generous hearts. —Acts 2:46b

Acts 2 lists the consequences of the first mighty outpouring of the Spirit. To be sure, there are miraculous signs by the apostles. But most of the list is taken up with the community life the believers experienced. At least from this passage, it seems the real sign of Pentecost was the explosion of sharing, gathering, hospitality, and sincerity—all infused with worship. Believers readily gave their wealth away. The public rewarded this eruption with "good will," and many joined this prophetic community.

We live in a society where privacy and self-sufficiency are tenets of faith and where loneliness abounds. This poverty is manifest when even our churches cater to individual needs and tolerate fragmentation. Are we open to rediscovering true community, as more homes are opened in hospitality, more stories shared, more communion bread broken, and more differences celebrated? What a sign that would be to the world! —*Byron Rempel-Burkholder*

Holy Spirit, enable the church to proclaim anew, in its life together, God's kingdom of love, healing, and hope.

4

Faithful servants

ACTS 6:1-15; 7:51-60

* *

Opening

Think about a time you were involved in a conflict. Who was involved? Was it a disagreement with those close to you or a dispute with those outside your community? Jot down your thoughts and feelings from that experience or draw them with colors. What were the positive and negative outcomes of this conflict?

Understanding God's Word

The church, still centered in Jerusalem, is growing rapidly. In response the religious establishment feels increasingly threatened and looks for ways to silence this new movement. The apostles are put in prison but freed when an angel opens the prison door.

The rapid growth of the church also creates tensions within the community of believers. A group of widows complains that they are not receiving their fair share of the food distribution. This disagreement is settled when the apostles suggest selecting seven deacons who will devote their time to serving at tables.

* *

For the leader

1. These passages highlight both internal and external conflict experienced by the early church. Invite the group to share the first words that come to mind when they hear the word "conflict." Or invite someone to share about an experience of conflict and how they responded to the questions in the opening.

2. This passage divides into three segments: Acts 6:1-7; 6:8-15; 7:51-60. Since the first segment deals with the conflict over food distribution, read it before "Conflict and the calling of more leaders" below. The second two segments can precede "The church's first martyr," which follows.

Acts 6:1-15; 7:51-60

One of those elected is Stephen. In addition to his faithful distribution work, he is also an effective evangelist. Stephen's evangelistic zeal leads to his death and to severe persecution that scatters the believers. The stoning of Stephen becomes a watershed moment for the church as it moves out of Jerusalem and begins embracing Gentiles.

Connecting with God's Word

Conflict and the calling of more leaders

The dissent that erupted over the distribution of food was ethnic in nature. Although all believers were still Jews, some were ethnic Jews whose ancestors had lived in Judea or Galilee for centuries. They were the Hebrews, more likely to speak Hebrew or Aramaic and more likely to follow traditional Jewish practices. The other believers were Hellenistic Jews, from outside of Palestine and more likely to speak Greek. The Hellenists were newcomers and not readily accepted by those who felt they owned their faith.

To their credit, the twelve did not ignore the problem. They proposed that seven assistants be selected to attend to the material needs of the entire body. One of those was Stephen; another is identified as a proselyte (a Gentile who had converted to Judaism). All seven had Greek names, indicating that this group was composed entirely of Hellenists, no doubt to complement the Hebrew apostles.

With this issue resolved, Luke notes that the movement continued to grow. Even many priests became convinced that Jesus was the Messiah and joined this new expression of faith.

- How does your congregation handle disagreement and conflict? How is conflict both a danger and an opportunity?

- This disagreement in the early church led to calling forth new leadership and resulted in continued church growth. Identify a comparable situation today in your congregation or the wider church.

- Our society is becoming increasingly diverse—culturally, racially, ethnically, etc. How is this affecting our worship, our denominational meetings, and our outreach? When have there been difficulties in working together, and when have you experienced the richness of broader fellowship?

- Are we willing to accept leadership from various ethnic and racial groups? How does this promote and energize the gospel's witness?

The church's first martyr

Not everyone was interested in hearing the good news about Jesus. Members of the synagogue of the Freedmen started an argument with Stephen. The Freedmen were Greek-speaking Jews and former slaves who had moved to Jerusalem. They were very loyal and closely connected to the traditions of the temple.

They charged Stephen with speaking against the temple and the law, both at the very heart of Judaism. This new faith in Jesus challenged the traditions and the foundations of their faith and identity.

Similarities to Jesus' trial and execution are striking. Both relied on false witnesses, and both involved blasphemy charges. As with Jesus' crucifixion, a mob mentality took over and justice was perverted. Like Jesus, Stephen was put to death outside of the city. Stephen's final words were also reminiscent of Jesus as he prayed, "Lord Jesus, receive my spirit."

- The story of Anabaptist martyrs is well documented in the *Martyrs Mirror*. This work was meant to inspire believers to faithful witness to Jesus. Initially martyrdom was an evangelistic witness that resulted in many converts. But with time the constant pressure of fleeing for one's life brought weariness and desire for a quiet, peaceful life. How has the history of martyrdom shaped Anabaptist Mennonites? To what extent is it part of our collective consciousness? How does it shape our witness today?

- Persecution did not stop at the end of the reformation. There are still countries in which it is illegal to convert to Christianity. How can Christians in Canada and the United States be supportive of Christians in other parts of the world who are being persecuted for their faith?

- Many Christians live in violent situations and realize they need to proclaim Jesus as the Prince of Peace. Mennonite church leaders in Africa ask why our missionaries have been so often silent about Jesus' way of peace and nonviolence. Does our history of persecution make us afraid to challenge the state over the use of military action? Do we fear renewed rejection? Or are we afraid it will hinder our evangelistic outreach? Why is our peace witness so often lacking when we invite people to make a faith commitment to Jesus?

Closing

Sing "Faith of the Martyrs" (number 413 in *Hymnal: A Worship Book*) or read together number 153 in *Sing the Journey*.

DEVOTIONALS

* *

Devotional 1

The Hellenists complained . . . because their widows were being neglected. —Acts 6:1

Nearly two thousand years ago the young church was coming to a grinding halt in a conflict over cultural differences, social status, and basic necessities. No doubt some people were silent. Some wanted to deny the problem while others wanted to force the issue. Those who sought a third way tried to raise their voices above those who argued loudly over differences.

Even then God was at work. Under the discernment of the apostles, the church called forth a new ministry. The ministry of deacons still exists to serve the needs of those who are suffering.

When we call on God, conflict can enable us to move on to the next lesson, the next miracle, the next manifestation of God's Holy Spirit. How many of our shared hardships, when brought prayerfully to God, could result in new opportunities to serve the body, encourage the humble, and build up the church of Christ? *—Craig Morton*

God, you have reconciled us to yourself through your Son, Jesus. Draw us together so we can serve each other and reach out to a needy world.

Devotional 2

Select from among yourselves seven men of good standing, full of the Spirit and of wisdom, whom we may appoint to this task. —Acts 6:3

"I don't like the word *power*," a friend said. "Power means oppression and might, and often leads to violence." Yet God's power of love is made real in its ability to change lives. Such power can counter the messages of our society that find power in money, status, or force.

How did the early church view power? According to this text, it chose seven deacons to take up the important responsibility of serving those in need. This model matched the example of Jesus, who fed the hungry, healed the sick, cast out debilitating spirits, and washed the feet of his disciples.

How do we choose church leaders today? Do we look for the most persuasive preacher, the administrator who promises the most for our money? Or do we look first at the heart: are they filled with the Holy Spirit, and do they act in God's love and wisdom? *—Elizabeth Raid*

God, may we be faithful servants of Christ, empowered to serve and spread your Word.

Devotional 3

Stephen, full of grace and power, did great wonders and signs among the people.
—Acts 6:8

Acts is about the expanding witness of the early church. The Holy Spirit empowered Christ's followers to bear witness beyond the Jewish faith. The message of Christ was for the whole world. God's reign had begun here on earth. "The kingdom of God is among you," Jesus had said (Luke 17:21b).

Stephen presented the gospel message in a powerful way. He knew his audience, the prideful religious leaders. As Paul did, he used his gift of speech to proclaim the work of God throughout history and culminating in Jesus the Christ. This led to his arrest and false accusation.

How am I articulating God's presence and powerful possibilities for living in love and faithfulness? Do my actions speak about God's love for all humanity? Do I express my faith in teaching, writing, comforting, confronting, and investing and managing resources for the benefit of all?
–Elizabeth Raid

In whatever arena you give me for witnessing, God, may I follow Stephen's example and boldly articulate my faith, no matter what the outcome.

* * * * * * * * * * * * * *

Devotional 4

They could not withstand the wisdom and the Spirit with which [Stephen] spoke.
—Acts 6:10

Stephen performed many miracles and worked hard to spread the good news of Jesus. This great pillar of the early church also created friction between himself and traditional Jewish leaders. Some may have been jealous of his power and fame. Others probably thought he was spreading lies and blasphemy. Yet when confronted by skeptics, Stephen boldly stood up for what he knew was right, and no one could stand against his words.

The writer of Acts makes clear that Stephen's power came from the Holy Spirit. The same Holy Spirit lives inside us. We have access to the same power and wisdom, and God will not leave us stranded when we feel unable to do what God wants us to do. James 1:5 says, "If any of you is lacking in wisdom, ask God, who gives to all generously and ungrudgingly, and it will be given you." *–Helen Balzer*

Thank you, God, for models of faith such as Stephen. Thank you also for the promise of your wisdom and power.

* * * * * * * * * * * * * *

Devotional 5

Yet the Most High does not dwell in houses made with human hands. —Acts 7:48a

In this address to the high priest's council, Stephen reminded them that God had been with the people of Israel throughout their history. God had walked with Abraham, Joseph, Moses, and the ancestors in the wilderness.

In all that time, God had not asked for a temple. Indeed, how could God dwell in a house when God had created all things? How could God be confined to one place, one people?

No wonder they became angry. Their identity, economy, and worship centered on the temple and its sacrifices. How dare

Acts 6:1-15; 7:51-60

Stephen remind them this was not what God really wanted!

What about us today? We do not have a temple, but we may still be tempted to think God dwells in our country, our church, our people in a special way. May we too remember that God is everywhere and loves everyone. *–Linda Gehman Peachey*

Dear God, thank you that you are not limited to one people or one place. You love us all. Help us to remember this always.

* * * * * * * * * * * * * *
Devotional 6

"Look," he said, "I see the heavens opened and the Son of Man standing at the right hand of God!" —Acts 7:56

Stephen, a deacon appointed to care for the needs of widows, orphans, and the poor, came into serious conflict with his co-religionists. His opponents couldn't refute his arguments, so they accused him of blasphemy, a crime punishable by death.

When they eventually cast him out of the city and stoned him, Stephen gave his persecutors—and us—much to think about. He placed his spirit into the hands of Jesus, becoming the first Christian martyr.

As a young pastor I felt very apprehensive in ministering at the time of death. But after being with a number of people at such times, I found an inexplicable peace in this ministry. Often the person dying would have a vision of heaven before death. Sometimes other family members shared the loved one's experience. These humbling, faith-building experiences are holy moments and provide a profound sense of unity with the eternal. *–Doug Snyder*

We give thanks for Stephen and his faith, and also for many we have known who have also looked into heaven by faith.

* * * * * * * * * * * * * *
Devotional 7

They covered their ears, and with a loud shout all rushed together against him. —Acts 7:57

When I have read this passage in the past, I have focused on Stephen and his example. This time I found myself wondering about the mob that stoned him. How could they? One phrase stuck out: "They covered their ears." When we cover our ears, we find ourselves doing things that would be unthinkable if we were listening.

What would I hear if I uncovered my ears? From time to time I read the newspaper or listen to the news as a prayer discipline. I try to listen more deeply than the words, and I ask myself how the people involved must have felt.

When I listen deeply, I am faced with the hard places in my heart that resist stretching. Listening requires me to change. It softens my heart, making me less judgmental and rigid. Uncovering our ears and listening to one another is essential to becoming compassionate, peaceful people. *–Susan Classen*

Uncover my ears, God of compassion, and open my heart so that I may know your truth.

Interpreting the Word

ACTS 8:26-38

* *

Opening

Recall a time when you were asked to do something new or something that stretched you beyond your comfort zone. How was God present with you? What did you learn about yourself, others, and God?

Understanding God's Word

This passage lifts up the ministry of Philip, another of the Hellenist leaders appointed in Acts 6. With the persecution that follows Stephen's death, many of the church leaders scatter. Philip goes to Samaria, where he has a successful ministry of teaching and healing.

This is a significant step since Jews and Samaritans have an uneasy relationship characterized by suspicion and even hostility. In Luke 9:51-56, for example, James and John want to call down fire from heaven when a Samaritan village refuses them hospitality.

When Philip arrives, however, these Samaritans receive the gospel eagerly. Indeed, the apostles in Jerusalem hear about the success of this ministry and send Peter and John to visit. Is this to check on what is happening? Whatever the case, they lend their encouragement to this mission and pray that these new believers might receive the Holy Spirit.

* *

For the leader

1. Summarize some of the background given below, especially about Philip, Jewish-Samaritan relationships, and the Ethiopian eunuch.

2. Ask four people to read the passage, playing the part of the narrator, the Spirit, Philip, and the eunuch.

In today's passage the Holy Spirit asks Philip to travel again, extending the gospel's reach even further beyond the ethnic Jewish family.

Connecting with God's Word

Explaining the good news

Following an angel's directive, Philip went into the wilderness and found an Ethiopian eunuch in his chariot, returning from a worship trip to Jerusalem. He was likely from the Nubian kingdom, which was not in modern Ethiopia but in Sudan. As a black African he was considered to be from "the ends of the earth." He was the treasurer for the queen of the Ethiopians and had great influence. As a God fearer he was attracted to Judaism, but his nationality and incomplete maleness made him an outsider (Deuteronomy 23:1).

The Ethiopian was reading from the prophet Isaiah, giving Philip an opportunity to start a conversation. The verses were from the fourth Servant Song in Isaiah 52:13–53:12. In the original context, it is not certain to whom Isaiah is referring: the prophet himself, the whole people of Israel, or the Messiah.

Many people had hoped the Messiah would be a glorious king like David. After the events of Good Friday, Jesus did not fit that messianic dream, but the disciples saw in this Servant Song a prophecy describing Jesus. In the suffering of Isaiah's servant, they found scriptural support for Jesus' suffering and death. Jesus did indeed fit the prophetic expectations of the Messiah after all.

Philip interpreted more than the passion of Jesus. He explained the "good news of Jesus" and put Jesus' death into its proper context. No doubt, he described Jesus' ministry of healing and casting out demons, his willingness to forgive sins, and his teachings about a life that pleases God. This had gotten Jesus into conflict with religious authorities who could not accept Jesus' claims of being God's Son. Eventually they put Jesus to death. But Jesus' death was not the end. God raised him back to life. The forces of evil were defeated, including that last enemy, death.

Philip invited the Ethiopian to believe and accept Jesus' gracious gift of forgiveness and reconciliation with God. He also explained the meaning of baptism: how he could become a member of God's family and no longer an outsider.

Philip's interpretation of the Scriptures helped the Ethiopian understand the God he had been searching for and worshiping. The Holy Spirit put in place what was needed for the final sealing of his new relationship with God. They saw some water and the Ethiopian requested baptism. As demonstrated in the waters of baptism, he was born anew.

- This account tells of another step in extending the gospel to people who would have been considered outsiders. How comfortable is your congregation with inviting "outsiders" to receive Jesus and join your church? What might be some barriers to welcoming people? How are you working to overcome them?

- Philip's ability to explain the Scriptures led to the Ethiopian's conversion to the way of Jesus. How do we equip ourselves to be more effective interpreters of the Word? How does your congregation strengthen members in their discipleship and witness?

Directed by God's Spirit

Throughout Acts, Luke reminds readers that it is the Holy Spirit who has given birth to the church and is guiding its spread to the ends of the earth Luke makes it clear that Philip was responding to the Holy Spirit's leading. The story begins with "an angel of the Lord said to Philip" and ends with "the Spirit of the Lord snatched Philip away." When Philip saw a chariot, the Spirit said to "go over to this chariot and join it."

This was a crucial moment in the life of the church. The first Gentile was baptized, and the door was opened for all people to be received into the church. The Spirit was directing every step.

- If our own witness and outreach is to be effective, it must also be Spirit directed, tuned to the Spirit's prompting. What are some ways you determine the Spirit's leading? Do you sense inner urgings? Discuss and discern with others? Study Scripture? Pray? How do you know when you are hearing the Spirit?

- How has the Spirit led you in surprising or unexpected ways? In those instances, what have you learned about God and God's will for you and others?

Closing

Sing "How Can We Be Silent" (number 61 in *Sing the Journey*). Conclude with benediction number 162 in *Sing the Journey*.

Acts 8:26-38

DEVOTIONALS

* *

Devotional 1

Then an angel of the Lord said to Philip, "Get up and go toward the south. . . ." So he got up and went. —Acts 8:26-27

An angel of the Lord pulled Philip from a successful mission in Samaritan villages to meet a lone traveler in the desert. Philip was so in tune with God's Spirit that he heard the call and obeyed the Spirit's direction. As he ran beside the chariot of the Ethiopian official, he recognized that the man was reading from the prophet Isaiah. Philip recognized that God was giving him an opportunity to share the gospel.

Across Africa, Anabaptist women are also being drawn to take bold opportunities. They study the Bible and share their gifts with the church. In their male-dominated contexts, these women theologians travel a lonely, desert road, but they have formed a network to support each other. They are eager to help guide others to greater understanding of God's Word. *—Ferne Burkhardt*

We give thanks, God, for the way your Spirit, in many ways, draws us to your call.

* * * * * * * * * * * * * * * *

Devotional 2

An angel of the Lord said to Philip, "Get up and go toward the south to the road that goes down from Jerusalem to Gaza." (This is a wilderness road.) —Acts 8:26

Philip was having a wonderful ministry in Samaria. He may have been ready to settle down for a long time. Then came this message from the angel, to go to a lonely road in the wilderness.

Even today that is a lonely stretch of highway. Besides Philip, only one person was on that road that day. But that one person came to faith in Christ, and he may have been the one who brought the gospel to Africa, where it has taken root and blossomed into vibrant faith.

Sometimes we may feel as though we are serving God in a wilderness: alone, obscure, with few people to serve and even fewer to notice. We may be a little tired of our wilderness. This passage reminds us to keep with the task at hand. God has something good going on, something we can't yet imagine, even in the wilderness. *—Jim Holm*

Whether in the wilderness or not, Lord, I believe you are at work in my life. Help me to continue faithfully, watching to see what you do.

* * * * * * * * * * * * * * * *

Devotional 3

An angel of the Lord said to Philip, "Get up and go toward the south to the road that goes down from Jerusalem to Gaza." (This is a wilderness road.) —Acts 8:26

It seems the Holy Spirit often draws us beyond our usual haunts, our settled views, our customary company. Philip's great virtue is that he listens for and takes seriously the urging of the Spirit to do the unexpected, the difficult, the inexplicable.

He goes south on the wilderness road. There he meets and serves an Ethiopian chief financial officer whose bold faith forever changes the shape of the church. The young churches of Africa never tire of hearing this story and reveling in the strength, joy, and dignity of this ancestral response to good news.

Philip would not normally be hanging about this stony road. And how could he attend to one who is so different? It all depends on Philip's willingness to be carried by the Spirit beyond the settled patterns of life. To make friends with the unpredictable. To be watchful, even in inconveniences, for the divine hand at work. —*Jonathan Larson*

Breathe on me breath of God, fill me with life anew, that I may love what thou dost love, and do what thou wouldst do.
—*Edwin Hatch*

* * * * * * * * * * * * * * *
Devotional 4

Philip began to speak, and starting with this scripture, he proclaimed to him the good news about Jesus. —Acts 8:35

Philip had already taken the gospel beyond Jewish communities to crowds of Samaritans, people with whom the Jews would not normally associate. Then God called him into the desert, where he explained the good news to an official from the Ethiopian court. Tradition says the Ethiopian became a missionary among his own people.

The gospel has continued to spread in unusual ways. In the 1920s and 1930s, for example, thousands of Mennonites fled persecution and death in Russia. Several thousand ended up in the wilds of the Chaco region of Paraguay.

Life was difficult during the early years, but they were able to establish successful communities. More importantly, they shared the gospel, both in the city and among aboriginal peoples. Today more than 21,000 Mennonites worship in German, Spanish, and indigenous languages in 150 congregations. Together they hosted the 2009 Mennonite World Conference. —*Ferne Burkhardt*

Help me, Lord, to be alert to opportunities to share the gospel today in creative ways.

* * * * * * * * * * * * * * *
Devotional 5

Philip began to speak, and starting with this scripture, he proclaimed to him the good news about Jesus. —Acts 8:35

"Our friend Nancy is studying with a cult group," my sister called to say. "What can we do? Let's ask God to direct us." Our prayers led me to invite Nancy for lunch. We shared the truth of Jesus and warned her about the deceptive teaching. As we talked she opened up: "I feel a spiritual battle raging inside me every day—a battle for my soul. I don't know what to believe."

God also nudged me to walk with her several times a week and give her a book about the false doctrines of this group. One morning she said, "I've renounced my association with their religion."

What good news! But Nancy needed further grounding. We attended a weekly Bible study and studied the Bible together. Just as Nancy searched for answers, so the Ethiopian official was seeking more understanding. God prompted Philip to meet this man and bring him living water.
—*Lydia E. Harris*

Almighty God, please make me sensitive to your Spirit's prompting so I will be available to tell others the good news of Jesus.

Acts 8:26-38

* * * * * * * * * * * * * * * *

Devotional 6

Philip began to speak, and starting with this scripture, he proclaimed to him the good news about Jesus. —Acts 8:35

As a child I recall walking to vacation Bible school with the neighbor children. I also remember things we learned from the Bible and its stories. Then there were missionary tales from Africa, India, and South America. I was fascinated by the idea of talking about Jesus with someone who had never heard the message before.

Here Philip and the Ethiopian official are traveling together on a desert road, deeply involved in the message of Isaiah 53 and discussing who this Messiah-figure of the Scriptures might be. It's a classic account of God bringing together two people in the right time at the right place.

My childhood missionary heroes went to faraway places, and this story also takes place in a distant land. But the message is for us where we are now. It's possible you may meet someone today who would like your company and insight to comprehend and respond to Jesus' call. *–Ken Seitz*

As you did for Philip and his desert acquaintance, Lord, bless me with the courage to live my life for you and share Jesus with those searching for answers.

* * * * * * * * * * * * * * * *

Devotional 7

Look, here is water! What is to prevent me from being baptized? —Acts 8:37

Do you remember the day you were baptized? I remember I was 14 years old and had a new dress for the occasion. The congregation sang "Happy Day" from the black church hymnal. I felt grown-up as a new member in the body of Christ.

Baptisms are joyous occasions. When our older daughter was baptized, I wished that my father could have been present. At our son's baptism—soon after we viewed a movie about Anabaptist leader Michael Sattler—I was grateful for a faith that had survived 500 years so that our children could be included. Our youngest daughter chose to be baptized on a church outing, with snowcapped Mount Hood as a backdrop.

It was a happy day for the Ethiopian. God had sent him a preacher by angel delivery. He probably told his friends back home so that they too became believers! *–Annie Lind*

Dear Father, Son, and Holy Spirit, keep me faithful to the covenant I made with you at my baptism.

New vision

ACTS 9:1-19A

* *

Opening

Many of us have not had a dramatic turn-around as Saul did. Yet we have likely experienced something that has made us rethink or change our minds. We may have had to change a behavior to improve the health of our bodies or relationships. Reflect on one of those experiences and what led you to make those changes. How has it affected your life? Are there other changes you feel called to make?

Understanding God's Word

This passage is rich in detail. Saul's animosity and persecution of believers fits with Acts 8:1-3. Scholars have been perplexed by Saul's visit to the Jewish high priest to receive documents for his persecution in Damascus, for there is little evidence that the Jerusalem high priest had authority over synagogues in Damascus. We can infer, however, that the Jesus movement had expanded into Syria.

This new movement is now being called "the Way" (see Acts 18:25; 19:9, 23; 22:4; 24:14, 22). Although Luke sometimes refers to "the church," most scholars believe the term *church* did not become associated with the Jesus movement until later in the first century.

* *

For the leader

1. What does the group know about Paul? Construct a group picture of him and some of the key events in his life. Include his contributions to the early church.

2. Ask everyone to read this passage silently and notice a phrase or image that especially stands out. You may want to do this in two sections, first focusing on verses 1-9 and then on verses 10-19a. Invite people to share brief responses.

While this passage is often called "the conversion of Paul," some interpreters—such as Beverly Roberts Gaventa in *From Darkness to Light: Aspects of Conversion in the New Testament* (Philadelphia: Fortress, 1986)—urge caution in applying this term here. Today *conversion* often means converting from one religion to another, with the assumption that all former beliefs are renounced.

That is not what happens to Saul. Prior to his encounter with the risen Lord, he is a Jew who does not believe Jesus is the Messiah. After this encounter he is a Jew who claims that Jesus *is* the Messiah and the Son of God. Paul also vigorously attempts to keep the Jesus movement connected to Judaism throughout his life. So it may be preferable to describe this as Saul's "transformative experience."

Connecting with God's Word

Encountering the risen Lord

Saul and his companions were headed toward Damascus, perhaps "breathing threats" even as they hiked. Suddenly and instantly, the scene and the world changed. Numerous elements in this account depict an encounter with divinity: Paul sees light from heaven, frequently associated with epiphanies or God's presence (Exodus 13:21; 20:18). And Paul hears his name twice, as Abraham, Jacob, Moses, and Samuel heard their names (Genesis 22:11; 46:2; Exodus 3:4; 1 Samuel 3:4).

A voice asked Saul, "Why do you persecute me?" Many commentaries note that the title "Lord" in Saul's inquiry "Who are you, Lord?" could have been akin to saying "sir" and did not yet reflect faith. But the response brought things to a head: "I am Jesus." As best we know, Saul never encountered Jesus "in the flesh," but now he encountered the risen Lord. Jesus went on to specify ". . . whom you are persecuting," emphasizing the tie between himself and the movement of believers.

Luke's note that others observed this episode assures readers that this encounter actually happened. The companions heard a voice but saw nothing. This corresponds to an Old Testament theme: God is too holy to be seen physically. It also correlates with Luke's interest in blindness versus "seeing with eyes of faith" (Luke 2:30; 4:18; 10:23-24; 24:16, 31; Acts 13:11; 28:27).

Saul's companions led him the rest of the way into Damascus, where he conducted a spiritual retreat, including a three-day fast. There he had more visions, for Saul foresaw someone helping him regain sight (Acts 9:12).

- What are the advantages and disadvantages of a dramatic conversion versus a gentle claiming? Does one make it easier to connect with others? What opportunities and dilemmas does each experience bring?

- How have you encountered God in your life? How were you changed in the process? How do you share your testimony with others?

"Not me, Lord!"

Ananias also had an encounter with the risen Lord. His initial response, "Here I am, Lord," is reminiscent of Genesis 22:1 and 1 Samuel 3:6, 8, where Abraham and Samuel hear God's call. But Ananias was reluctant. He knew well the persecutor's reputation. We can almost hear his dismay. Told to go to Judas's house and help Saul regain his sight, Ananias protested, "Not me, Lord!"

Ananias was terrified, but he did what he was commanded. He laid hands on Saul and announced that he was there to help Paul see again (we might add, "with eyes of new faith") and be filled with the Holy Spirit.

Those with access to the Old Testament Apocrypha will find a related reference to scales falling from eyes in Tobit 3:17; 11:13. Whatever the physical explanation, the person saw God and God's ways anew. Saul experienced *metanoia*—a total transformation. Recognizing this, he requested baptism, the same practice that started Jesus on his ministry and initiates each believer into a life of ministry. Saul was now on "the Way" . . . even as he gained vision and strength.

- Ananias receives little attention in church history. Yet he took quite a risk, leading to quite a result. Have you had any similar experiences where you felt called to step out on a limb and do something that felt potentially dangerous? How did you respond and what happened as a result?

- How do we know when to be cautious and when to step out in faith? How do we assess when God is calling us to be bold and when to be careful and avoid putting ourselves or others in danger? What signs tell us that God is speaking to us?

Closing

Sing "Amazing Grace" or "Open My Eyes, That I May See" (numbers 143 or 517 in *Hymnal: A Worship Book*).

Acts 9:1-19a

Devotionals

* *

Devotional 1

Saul, still breathing threats and murder against the disciples of the Lord, went to the high priest and asked him for letters.
—Acts 9:1-2

People tend to breathe hard when their deep convictions are challenged. I still recall a congregational meeting where a matter of discernment escalated into an emotional time bomb. At one point a participant could take it no longer and had to leave. His breathing was deep and rapid, as if he had just run a mile.

Our breathing is directly affected by our passion. Certainly Saul was ardent in his convictions. He cared so deeply, some would call him fanatical. It took a special light to harness that fervor and transform hate into love.

That light of transformation continues to burn today. My Christian brother who took himself out of that congregational meeting confided later he was embarrassed he had to leave. Yet he cared too much for the fragile cords of the body of Christ to risk bloodying them with an angry outburst. I believe he had been touched by that special light. *—Jon M. Yoder*

God, your breath is life. Take my passions and harness them to your will. Help me pay attention to my breathing, especially when I am breathing hard.

Devotional 2

[Saul] asked, "Who are you, Lord?" The reply came, "I am Jesus, whom you are persecuting." —Acts 9:5

As Saul traveled to Damascus to capture and kill Christians in that city, Jesus appeared to him and stopped him in his tracks. In time Saul the persecutor emerged as Paul the church planter and missionary.

God still has the power to change lives. Rocky was known as the meanest man on the mountain where he lived. When he had been drinking—and that was often because he owned the local bar—Rocky picked fights with anyone who crossed his path. His life was a series of barroom brawls and arrests for disorderly conduct.

But that all changed when Rocky met the Lord. Jesus changed him into a loving father and grandfather. Rocky sold his bar and told his former drinking buddies about his new life. One by one, as they observed the changes in him, they also came to know Jesus. Rocky, the meanest man on the mountain, became God's missionary.
—Nancy Witmer

Jesus, thank you for changing my life. Let me be a conduit of your life-changing love to the people I meet today.

* * * * * * * * * * * * * * *

Devotional 3

But get up and enter the city, and you will be told what you are to do. —Acts 9:6

In our leadership group at church, we've been thinking about Paul. If his conversion occurred today, there would be serious credibility questions. As one who had killed Christians and tried to wipe out the church, would he really expect us to believe he had a vision on the highway and suddenly became a believer? Would we really welcome him as an apostle and minister of the faith?

In today's church we are often concerned with professional qualifications for those called to ministry. Usually we have good reasons for this. We need to know if staff and volunteers will be reliable and honest, and that they won't pose a safety threat. But sometimes we play it too safe, being wary of someone who might threaten our comfort zones.

How do we react when God calls unlikely apostles and prophets to challenge us today? Are we willing to listen to unconventional words, from unconventional sources?
–Philip Wiebe

O God, I confess I prefer safe messages from safe messengers rather than challenging words from unconventional prophets and visionaries. Help me be open to your leading.

* * * * * * * * * * * * * * *

Devotional 4

But get up and enter the city, and you will be told what you are to do. —Acts 9:6

One of my refrigerator magnets shows a little boy sitting in a puddle, his face splattered with mud, and stars and spirals rising from his head. The caption reads, "Okay,

God! Now I'm ready to listen!"

Paul was zealously doing what he thought was right—what God wanted him to do. Meeting Jesus in a blinding vision literally stopped Paul in his tracks. There he was, flat on the dusty road to Damascus.

Finally, instead of doggedly doing what he thought was right, Paul was ready to ask, "Lord, what do you want me to do?" Temporarily unable to see with his eyes, he was ready to see with his spirit and soul—beyond his current understanding.

When we are ready to listen, God will bring about changes in our lives. God will set us in a new direction and do more than we can imagine in us and through us.
–Ruth Smith

Dear God, help me walk so closely to you that I can hear your gentle whisper rather than needing to be jerked out of my rut.

* * * * * * * * * * * * * * *

Devotional 5

Saul got up from the ground, and though his eyes were open, he could see nothing. —Acts 9:8a

Each of us is like an onion. Peel off the outer protective shell, and you come to the first layer, with a fairly tough skin. Peel this one and there is a second layer, and more layers after that, until you get to a tender central core.

Often the longer we live, the more sure we are of our belief systems. We pull that tough outer shell around ourselves and settle down, no longer looking for surprises. Sometimes, as Paul did, we attack those whose ideas threaten us.

God decided it was time to help Paul move down deeper into his own center. Paul needed first to know that he was blind. Isn't that the core of most religious conversions?

42   *Acts 9:1-19a*

We suddenly understand just how blind we have been. New life, new joy, new understanding is born as God leads us out of our blindness. –*Mary Lou Cummings*

God, there are layers deep down that I haven't surrendered to you. Show me the ways I prefer to be blind, and lead me by the hand toward healing and wholeness.

* * * * * * * * * * * * * *

Devotional 6

And he has come here with authority from the chief priests to arrest all who call on your name. —Acts 9:14 (NIV)

Most teenagers fantasize about heroic actions they might perform some day. But a group of young Christians in Ethiopia in the 1970s didn't feel at all heroic as they sat on the cold concrete floor of a prison cell. Not one of these teenagers had chosen this role. Yet God had chosen them to witness to the love and power of Jesus' resurrection.

Ananias didn't ask to be God's instrument either. Very few of us would want to help a potential traitor after all. Saul's conversion looked more like a trick than a true turn-around. But Ananias obeyed God. His first words to Paul were "Brother Saul." Ananias's fear gave way to love and welcome.

And in that prison in Ethiopia, each young person described a peace and strength they had never known before. God moves in mysterious ways to bring rebirth where there is darkness and despair—and God often does it through ordinary people. –*Mary Lou Cummings*

Let me be like Ananias, O God, so that I too may warmly bless others who need your healing. Let my fears fall away so that your love and power can move through me.

* * * * * * * * * * * * * *

Devotional 7

Ananias answered, "Lord, I have heard from many about this man, how much evil he has done to your saints . . ." But the Lord said to him, "Go." —Acts 9:13, 15

I remember a student who planned his research paper to prove a particular viewpoint. His research, however, led him to realize the opposite viewpoint had more credibility. He was open to the new ideas and information, and his paper eventually supported that side.

Acts 9 is the story of two calls, of two men stopped in their tracks and challenged to change their minds. Saul's encounter with Jesus may seem the more dramatic. But inside the city of Damascus, another man, Ananias, is also challenged to obey Jesus' voice.

Because Saul and Ananias both recognize the voice of the Lord, they are willing to change their minds. While I need to stand firm in my beliefs, not easily swayed by different opinions, I also need to be willing to change my mind when I see I am wrong. May God grant me that willingness. –*Janet Gehman*

God, when you want to challenge my opinions and call me to accept a different idea or interpretation, I want to be ready to obey.

Seeking help in times of need

ACTS 9:32-43

* *

Opening

This passage highlights the healing ministry of the early church as well as the way it cared for widows and others. How does your congregation continue these ministries? If possible, think of a time when the church was helpful to you in bringing healing or renewed life. What elements were especially helpful and life giving? What was not helpful?

Understanding the Word

The book of Acts is organized around Jesus' final words: "But you will receive power when the Holy Spirit comes upon you; and you will be my witnesses in Jerusalem, in all Judea and Samaria, and to the ends of the earth" (1:8).

The movement of the gospel of Jesus into Judea and Samaria begins in 8:5 with the missionary work of Philip. Lydda is a town northwest of Jerusalem. It isn't clear how there have come to be saints in Lydda for Peter to visit, but the town does lay in the path of Philip's route from Azotus to Caesarea (8:40). Perhaps the statement that Philip preached the gospel in all the towns along the way to Caesarea is no exaggeration.

Peter is the central figure in the story of the establishment of the gospel in Jerusalem. As the church spreads, the work of Philip and Saul/Paul is

* *

For the leader

1. Healing stories can be difficult to discuss, as many people do not experience physical healing. It is important to be sensitive and allow space for questions and discomfort about why people continue to suffer and die, and how God is present even in these situations.

2. Ask someone to read the passage in a dramatic way. If your group enjoys role-plays, ask them to act it out during the reading.

featured. With the church at peace and multiplying throughout the region (9:31), Peter returns to center stage, preparing us for the opening of the mission to the Gentiles in the story of Cornelius (chapter 10).

Connecting with God's Word

Jesus' healing ministry continued

As Peter had done earlier in Jerusalem, he continued to show that Jesus' ministry continues through those who speak and act in his name. The story of Peter's healing of Aeneas, a paralytic for eight years, echoes the account of Jesus' cure of the paralytic in Luke 5:24-26, including the command to "get up" and to "make your mat." Peter had learned from his master and now ministered with Jesus' power.

While in Lydda, Peter was summoned by Christians in nearby Joppa. A disciple named Tabitha had taken ill and died. This is the only time in the New Testament that a woman is referred to as a disciple. Clearly she was a special person, one whose acts on behalf of the poor had made her renowned in the Christian community in Joppa.

The miracle in Joppa echoed even more closely one of Jesus' miracles: the raising Jairus's daughter (Luke 8:49-56). Once Tabitha opened her eyes, Peter helped her to her feet and presented her to the "saints and widows."

Later in church history the widows became a special order devoted to good works and charity on behalf of the poor. Certainly their patron saint could have been Dorcas/Tabitha, a disciple returned to life by the power of God.

True, this was resuscitation rather than resurrection. Tabitha, as Lazarus and Jairus's daughter, would face death again. But the deed proclaimed more loudly than any words that nothing has been withheld from the church, not even power over death.

- Healing stories like these can be difficult for those who suffer from long-term illness, or for family members whose loved ones were not healed or restored to life. How do you understand healing? Is it primarily a physical healing from the illness or impairment itself? Or can aspects of healing be found through worship, through friendship, or in other ways? What examples of healing have you experienced or witnessed?

- We don't generally think of Tabitha's work as a healing ministry, and yet it may have felt as important to the widows she served as the physical healings Peter enabled. Should we think more intentionally about care for the vulnerable as healing work? How are these ministries similar or different?

Many believed in the Lord

Miracles in the New Testament often have what could be called an ulterior motive. John's gospel calls them "signs," authentications of who Jesus was and why he came. In Acts, miracle stories are often followed by statements of their effect—how many "saw" and "heard" and subsequently "turned to the Lord" and "believed."

But whatever use the writers make of them, we should not miss what the miracles actually did, and for whom they did it. They were not arbitrary wonders or magic publicity tricks but acts of compassion on behalf of those in need. The miracles restored health, alleviated pain, made people whole, and drew attention to the power and compassion of God.

And so must we. Whether or not anyone will discern a supernatural dimension in our actions or their results, we must continue to act in the name of Jesus, bringing healing and life. The ministries of the disciple Tabitha and the miracles of the apostle Peter, both done in Jesus' name, were equally faithful demonstrations of the power of a compassionate God.

- Neither story in today's text involves any preaching of the gospel, yet both result in widespread conversions. In what situations are actions more persuasive than words?

- Tabitha's friends showed Peter evidence of her work and told him stories of her charity on behalf of others. Such demonstrations and stories are often said to make up our legacy, the evidence we leave behind of the kind of life we have lived. Consider this legacy for:

  - Yourself

  - A person you know whose gifts have not been adequately recognized

  - Your congregation in the last 10 years

Closing

Sing "Healer of Our Every Ill" (number 377 in *Hymnal: A Worship Book*) or "Christ's Is the World" (number 62 in *Sing the Journey*).

DEVOTIONALS

* *

Devotional 1

"Jesus Christ heals you; get up and make your bed." And immediately [Aeneas] got up. —Acts 9:34 (NIV)

At an Iroquois Nation gathering, I watched as men, women, and children danced together following a long prayer to the Creator of life. These folks modeled resurrection for me. In the face of injustice and a painful history, they chose new life, hope, and community over despair.

Acts 9 shares a number of resurrection stories. For Aeneas, paralyzed in bed for eight years, it was restored health. For Tabitha it was returning to life after death. For Simon the tanner, whose job rendered him ritually unclean, it was Peter's acceptance and willingness to stay in his home.

In each case, Jesus Christ was the great healer. Jesus invites us to let him help us conquer the pain of the past, the paralysis, the dead hopes. Peter, the one who often didn't get it, now became the agent of healing for others, the one who could point the hurting ones toward Jesus' power.
—Mary Lou Cummings

God, heal the wounded. Raise up those who need your love today. Use your children as agents of healing. And let me too experience resurrection power.

Devotional 2

All the residents of Lydda . . . saw him and turned to the Lord. —Acts 9:35

Soon after moving to Beirut, we were introduced to Hicham. As a teenager he had joined one of the militias that would shoot at enemies across Beirut's Green Line. But one day he simply could not pull the trigger on an elderly woman.

A spiritual awakening was taking root within. After reading Jesus' words about loving the enemy, Hicham gave up hatred and embraced a call to preach reconciliation in war-torn Beirut.

Sometimes he teams up with a fellow believer who has also experienced a spiritual awakening to forsake violence. As the residents of Lydda, these men have turned to the Lord. Now they go about Lebanon announcing God's work in their hearts and lives.

Such is the pattern of life we are called to. As we tune in to the healing power of Jesus, we are transformed and find ourselves sharing the good news wherever we go. *—Ken Seitz*

God, we give praise for Peter—an instrument in helping others turn to you—and for those today who are stirred, as Hicham was, to reorder their lives toward your peace.

* * * * * * * * * * * * * * *

Devotional 3

In Joppa there was a disciple whose name was Tabitha, which in Greek is Dorcas. She was devoted to good works and acts of charity. —Acts 9:36

From the witness of friends, it was clear Dorcas's witness through needle and thread had made its mark. Dorcas has inspired many Christians in sewing circles today, many of which bear her name. Each spring our church displays handiwork made by the Dorcas Circle for the annual Mennonite Central Committee sale, which raises money for relief and service programs around the world.

As Dorcas's friends did, we can't help but admire generous disciples who use their talents to help others and witness to their faith. When God raised her from the dead, God provided Dorcas with a second opportunity to be a witness. Her new life was itself a witness of God's love and power.

How are you witnessing with your words, works, and being at this stage in your life? Are your neighbors drawn to Christ by seeing God at work in you and through you?
–Susan Miller Balzar

God, may the work of my hands, the words of my mouth, and the evidence of my new life in Christ help many people to believe in you.

* * * * * * * * * * * * * * *

Devotional 4

In Joppa there was a disciple whose name was Tabitha, which in Greek is Dorcas. She was devoted to good works and acts of charity. —Acts 9:36

Luke emphasizes the leadership of New Testament women. Like Mary Magdalene, Joanna, and Susanna (Luke 8:2-3), Dorcas

was renowned for caring for the needs of believers. We do well to recognize and celebrate such faith heroes who use their gifts to lead and serve Christ's body.

In 2005 a group of us met Maria Gloria Penayo de Duarte in Asunción, Paraguay. Wife of President Nicanor Duarte Frutos, Gloria shared her faith pilgrimage. She told us she had resisted her husband's presidential candidacy, wanting to avoid media attention. Soon, however, she sensed God calling her to use her position for good. She not only witnesses to her faith and leads women's Bible studies, but she has also galvanized her church's outreach through a ministry to a hundred homeless youth. A rehab center helps them get off drugs and into school.

As Dorcas did, Maria Gloria Penayo provides a model of caring for Christ and his people. *–Lynn Jost*

Thank you, Jesus, for strong models of faithful service and leadership in the church. Help us to learn from them and follow their example today.

* * * * * * * * * * * * * * *

Devotional 5

All the widows stood beside him, weeping and showing tunics . . . that Dorcas had made. —Acts 9:39b

I confess that my image of Dorcas has been that of someone at a sewing machine, much like women today who enjoy sewing. It is helpful to remember that in Dorcas's time all of this would have been done by hand, perhaps starting with the flax or wool itself. Making clothes was a long and time-consuming effort, which meant that they were scarce and precious. Even as recently as the 1800s, clothing items were listed in people's wills because of their value.

Perhaps this explains the devotion of these widows to Dorcas. With no social security or employment options, they likely lived hand to mouth. They had no extra resources for things like clothes when they wore out. Clearly Dorcas helped meet a deep and heart-felt need.

Today clothing is more abundant, yet people continue to struggle for basic necessities. Who in your community is helping make sure these needs are met? —Linda Gehman Peachey

Dear God, thank you for the witness of people like Dorcas, who share their labor and resources with others. Help us follow their example.

* * * * * * * * * * * * * * * * *

Devotional 6

He turned to the body and said, "Tabitha, get up." Then she opened her eyes, and seeing Peter, she sat up. —Acts 9:40b

Miracles are signs that the kingdom of God is breaking into this earthly realm. The miracles in the book of Acts are signs that Jesus is alive and at work through people like Peter who faithfully follow Jesus. Tabitha's resurrection gave Peter credibility as a disciple of Jesus. More importantly, it was a sign that Jesus still had the power to reverse death.

Until Christ's return, we still face the consequence of sin and the reality of death. The good news is that the journey into death takes us into the presence of our resurrected Lord.

Tabitha's resurrection resulted in many coming to confess Jesus as Lord. Signs of the kingdom always draw people to Jesus. A challenge for us today is to recognize signs of the kingdom, and then draw people's attention to what God is doing in our world.

Jesus is alive and still transforms lives. What signs will we see today? —Michael Dick

Lord Jesus, give me eyes of faith to see the miracles you are doing in the world around me.

* * * * * * * * * * * * * * * * *

Devotional 7

[Peter] gave her his hand and helped her up. —Acts 9:41a

Although we don't know the names of most recipients of healing in the New Testament, Aeneas and Tabitha are named. This helps them stand out as likely leaders in their churches.

Aeneas is assumed to be one of the saints of Lydda. Tabitha is described more fully, especially in her life of charity. Although details of the internal life of the early church are scanty, the narrator emphasizes her sharing of wealth with the needy in the church and her provision of garments for widows.

As the church moved into new areas, Christ's disciples expressed active concern for the needy. People like Tabitha showed the power of the gospel through lives "devoted to good works and acts of charity" (9:36).

What acts of charity have we received from loved ones or neighbors today? What charity have we offered? —Patty Friesen

Help us to help each other, Lord, each other's load to bear, that all may live in true accord, our joys and pains to share.
—Charles Wesley

8

Never alone

Acts 12:1-17

* *

Opening

Today's story is an engaging one about the power of prayer and about God's deliverance in the face of King Herod's opposition. Yet it is also difficult, in that God does not always intervene to rescue people. Stephen and James were both martyred and many innocent people continue to suffer violence and persecution today. How do you resolve this dilemma between faith and reality? What especially troubles you? How might God be present even in situations that end in pain and death?

Understanding God's Word

This is the second time Peter is in prison and then released through the intervention of an angel (Acts 5:17-20). In this imprisonment two opposing forces are at work. First is Herod's desire to strengthen his political power by appeasing the Jews who want the disciples persecuted and even killed. But Herod's power is no match for God's power unleashed by the Christian community. It fervently prays for Peter's release.

King Herod Agrippa I is the grandson of Herod the Great and nephew of Herod Antipas. It was Herod Antipas who executed John the Baptist and

* *

For the leader

1. This passage focuses on Peter and on the praying church. Ask two people to read it on opposite sides of the room. While the first reads verses 1-11, have everyone put themselves in Peter's shoes. What was he thinking and feeling? As verses 12-17 are read, try to imagine what those believers were experiencing.

2. As noted in the opening, this lesson opens up difficult questions, especially when something terrible happens and it appears God is not answering our prayers. Explore how God is present in those situations.

whom Jesus referred to as "that fox." The Herodian family reacts brutally to anyone who challenges their power. The killing of the male children in Bethlehem at the time of Jesus' birth is but one example.

Now Herod Agrippa has just killed the apostle James. Hoping to gain even more favor with the Jews, he also goes after Peter. Peter is arrested during the festival of Unleavened Bread, the same festival during which Jesus was arrested and executed.

As Peter sits in prison he surely reflects upon his time with Jesus. He remembers the Passover night when Jesus shared the bread and wine, and when he denied his Lord. He also remembers the lakeshore breakfast when the resurrected Jesus forgave him and commissioned him to feed his flock. Now he faces his own death.

Connecting with God's Word

Peter's deliverance

Peter's wrists were chained to two soldiers. Two more soldiers guarded the door. It was the night before Peter was to face Herod and certain death. An angel appeared and woke Peter from a deep sleep. This is not the picture of a prisoner gripped by fright. The peace of God was with him. The chains fell off, and Peter followed the angel until he was out of prison.

It was not until he was on the street that the magnitude of what God had done hit Peter. The Passover was a celebration of God's deliverance. Peter stood on the street in awe, knowing that God had also delivered him. Herod's evil schemes were defeated, just as those of Pharaoh had been. Neither king could match the power of God.

- Give examples of how God has done the unexpected in your life or the life of another. What happened and who was involved?

- Usually we think of angels as supernatural beings. Is this always the case, or are there times when God uses people to act as "angels" and help bring deliverance?

The praying church

Peter went to the house of Mary, the mother of John Mark. Peter had a very special relationship with Mark and called him "my son" (1 Peter 5:13). It was Mark who wrote one of the gospels, likely using Peter as his source.

Mary's house may have been the location of the upper room where Jesus and the disciples had celebrated the Passover and later waited for the outpouring of the Holy Spirit. Now many Christians gathered there to pray. They were using intercessory prayer, the only power they had to deal with Herod.

In a humorous account Luke reports how the servant girl Rhoda recognized Peter's voice but was so overjoyed she forgot to open the gate. Instead she ran back to announce the good news that Peter was standing outside. These believers, who were praying for Peter's deliverance, found it hard to believe their prayers had been answered.

Rhoda faced the same skepticism as the women who had told the disciples that Jesus was risen. They had dismissed it as an "idle tale" and "did not believe them" (Luke 24:11). But Rhoda insisted and Peter was allowed to enter the house. The power of prayer had prevailed.

- What do you believe about intercessory prayer? We know that fervent prayer does not always cure illness, overcome an addiction, prevent a marriage breakup, avert an accident, or prevent financial bankruptcy. So what is prayer and how does it work?

- Think about times when you or the church community prayed for others. What was the outcome for the person for whom prayer was offered? How did it affect your relationship with God? How do you respond when it appears your prayers are not answered?

- Name situations today where people have relied on prayer, nonviolence, and the power of God's love to bring about change. Who was involved and what did they do? What was the result?

Closing

Read or sing together "My Soul Cries Out" (number 124 in *Sing the Story*). Pray together number 154 in *Sing the Journey*.

DEVOTIONALS

*   * * * * * * * * * * * * * * * * * *

Devotional 1

While Peter was kept in prison, the church prayed fervently to God for him. —Acts 12:5

Recently we attended a special service of Sudanese Christians living in Beirut. As these believers from half a dozen congregations across the city shared in the service, we heard prayers offered for those in prison. We know dozens of persons, often bread-winners, in prison for violation of immigration laws. These Sudanese Christians faithfully visit those in jail and practice mutual aid. With help from Mennonite Central Committee and other groups, they try to provide for the inmates' families.

Today our Sudanese brothers and sisters are part of a global community of believers who experience hardship and even prison in their homeland and often as well in lands where they seek refuge. Like the early church's prayer for Peter, our support for these Christians begins with prayer not only for their release but also for the advance of God's purpose through their lives.
–Ken Seitz

Remind us, Lord, of your faithful witnesses who suffer in prison. May you watch over them and bring release.

Devotional 2

Suddenly an angel of the Lord appeared and a light shone in the cell. He tapped Peter on the side and woke him, saying, "Get up quickly." And the chains fell off his wrists. —Acts 12:7

We may think that little in our lives could compare to Peter's dramatic rescue from his prison cell. Maybe, however, we should think again. Prisons of despair, hopelessness, and difficult situations can also close in on us, but they need not confine us. The vision of God's salvation and help provides the catalyst for significant, even extraordinary change.

Therapists talk about "visualization" as the action and energy we bring to difficult circumstances. With visualization we refuse to be imprisoned by the moment, instead focusing our minds on change for good that can come in our situation.

For believers, vision starts with prayer—prayer which dares to see God's Spirit as the freeing, transforming power that unlocks the prison. To encourage and empower people to believe and have vision is to assist them in bending back the iron bars that surround them. *–Doug Snyder*

Whatever limitations or prisons I feel, God, let them be tested in the light of your will and purposes for me. Let me pray and live with expectation of release and freedom.

* * * * * * * * * * * * * *
Devotional 3

The angel said to [Peter], "Fasten your belt and put on your sandals. . . . Wrap your cloak around you and follow me."
—Acts 12:8

The angel's words to Peter, "Get up" and "follow me," are not a first for him. Years earlier Jesus himself called him to leave his fishing business and become a disciple. This time it is a command to gain miraculous release from prison.

The angel's summons to Peter reflects the urgency of the situation: "Let's get out while we have an opportunity!" Doors and gates literally open. Peter, in a daze, walks to freedom. The passage concludes with Peter's reaffirmation of faith—contrasting sharply with his denial of Jesus on the eve of the crucifixion.

God's call comes in many forms. It may not be as straightforward as it was for Peter. But wherever we are in the world, serving God in whatever manner, we are continuously called as followers of "the Way" (Acts 9:2). As we accept the call with whatever light we have, we find true freedom.
–Ken Seitz

God, in the midst of competing calls and invitations, aid us in discerning when to get up and follow, when to wait, and when to say no.

* * * * * * * * * * * * * *
Devotional 4

[Peter] went to the house of Mary . . . where many had gathered and were praying.
—Acts 12:12

This story has always been a favorite, partly because it is so typical of human nature.

I easily identify with Rhoda, the maid who answered the knock. Upon hearing Peter's voice, she ran back inside without opening the door. But those praying could not believe their prayers had been answered. Poor Rhoda! "You are out of your mind." After persistent knocking, Peter was finally admitted.

I'm reminded of visits with the directors of a home for street children in Beirut. John and Lena speak easily of answers to prayer for the daily needs of their institution, which serves over 80 children. During a recent visit, we met a wealthy supporter. Later that evening John told us how the woman had spontaneously left a signed check for them to fill in the needed amount to cover a group of expenses. God hears and answers prayers for these abandoned children and those who care for them. *–Ken Seitz*

Poet James Montgomery wrote, "Prayer is the Christian's vital breath, the Christian's native air." Thank you, Lord, for opportunities to pray.

* * * * * * * * * * * * * *
Devotional 5

Suddenly an angel of the Lord appeared and a light shone in the cell. —Acts 12:7a

I have always thought this angel was an otherworldly figure, sent by God to rescue Peter. But it is also intriguing to wonder if this could have been someone in the prison, perhaps a guard who had been touched by Peter's testimony and could not bear to see him killed. Could someone like this have come with a candle to guide Peter out of prison?

To me such a possibility is even more miraculous than an angel from heaven, for it signals there might have been followers of "the Way"—or at least sympathizers—even in

Herod's prison. Even there, someone was willing to lead a daring escape in response to God's nudging.

We know God works through people. Sometimes we call them angels, especially when they are strangers who help out in times of need. These angels remind us that God's love reaches everywhere, even where we least expect. *—Linda Gehman Peachey*

Thank you, God, for angels, whether from heaven or earth. Thank you for their willingness to help in times of need, even when it's risky.

* * * * * * * * * * * * * * * *

Devotional 6

They said to her, "You are out of your mind!" —Acts 12:15a

How quickly these believers discounted Rhoda! "You're out of your mind." "It is his angel." No one even bothered to go and see if what she said was true. This was even more dismissive than when the women disciples reported Jesus' resurrection. At least that time Peter went to the tomb to investigate.

Why was it so hard to believe these women? Was it because women were not considered reliable witnesses? Or were their messages just so unexpected and unbelievable?

On the one hand, these vignettes are distressing for what they say about gender dynamics in the early church. On the other hand, they seem to poke fun at the leading disciples, asking why it was so hard for them to believe. They remind us that sometimes the model disciples are not the ones we expect. Sometimes it's the women and the servants who see the truth first and help lead the way. *—Linda Gehman Peachey*

God, give us humble hearts, willing to hear your surprising news from all your disciples. Help us pay attention to what they have to tell us.

* * * * * * * * * * * * * * * *

Devotional 7

Meanwhile Peter continued knocking; and when they opened the gate, they saw him and were amazed. —Acts 12:16

I was surprised when a speaker at a conference asked how many people believed we would be able to achieve the goals we were seeking. A few raised their hands, but most of us did not. Many were pessimistic that we could make enough changes to significantly reduce the culture of violence in our society.

The speaker went on to ask how we expected others to join us if we ourselves didn't really believe this work would succeed. How could we keep working if we didn't expect it would make much difference?

These are difficult questions, asking us how we maintain faith while being realistic about the likely outcome. No doubt those praying for Peter felt a similar tension. They prayed with all their hearts yet dared not hope too much. They had trouble believing, just as we do, even when the miracle they hoped for appeared before them. *—Linda Gehman Peachey*

Dear God, we want to believe; we want to trust that your power of love will transform and redeem all things. O God, help our unbelief! Help us keep trusting even when we cannot see the end.

CPSIA information can be obtained at www.ICGtesting.com
Printed in the USA
BVOW010620140213

313209BV00007B/41/P